MISS SWEET POTATO PIE AND THE SOUL FOOD BABIES

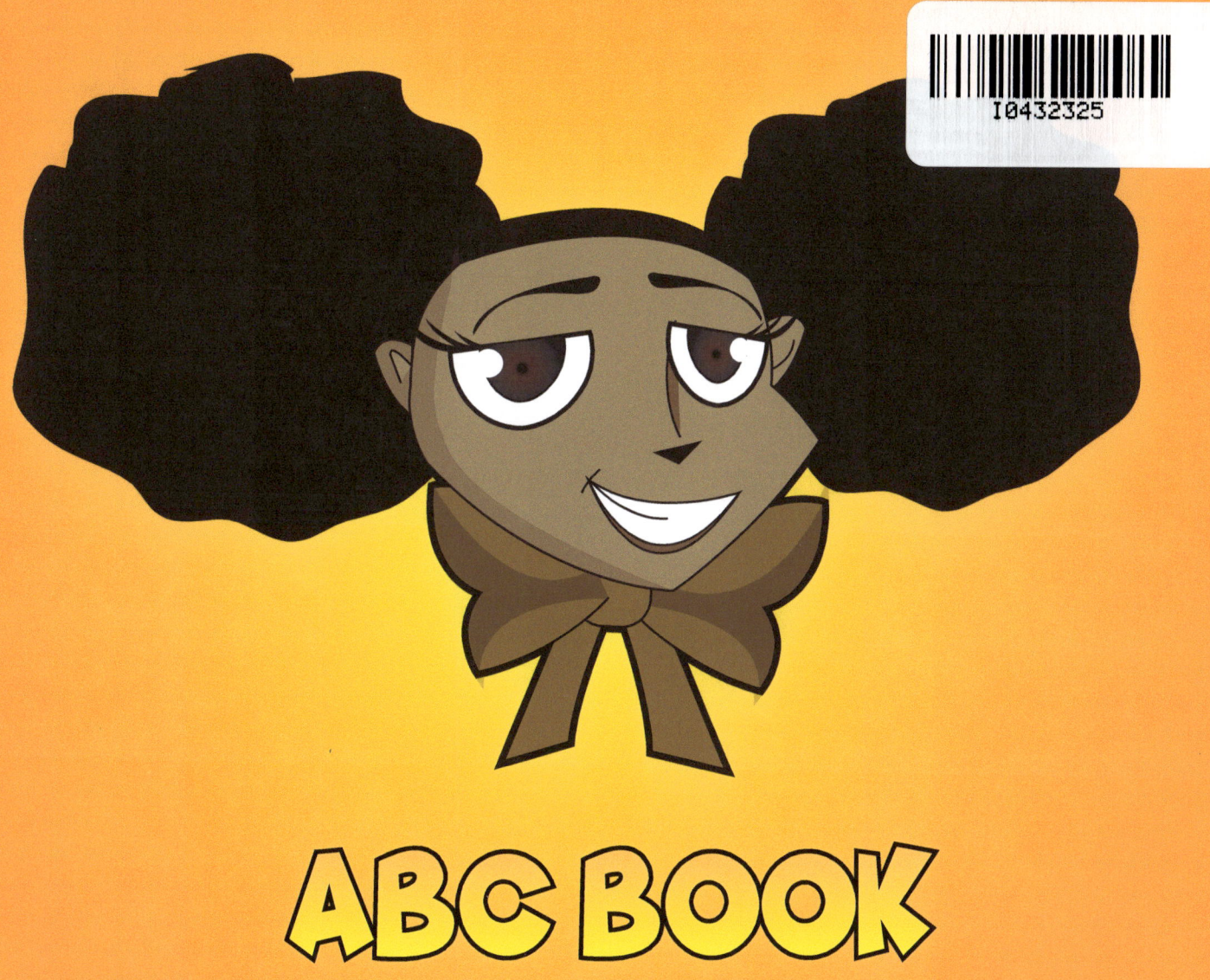

ABC BOOK

Copyright 2019 by Dianne Snowden Johnson

All rights reserved. No part of this book may be reproduced, transmitted or stored in an information retrieval system in any form or by any means, graphic, electronic, or mechanical, including photocopying, taping, and recording without prior written permission from the author.

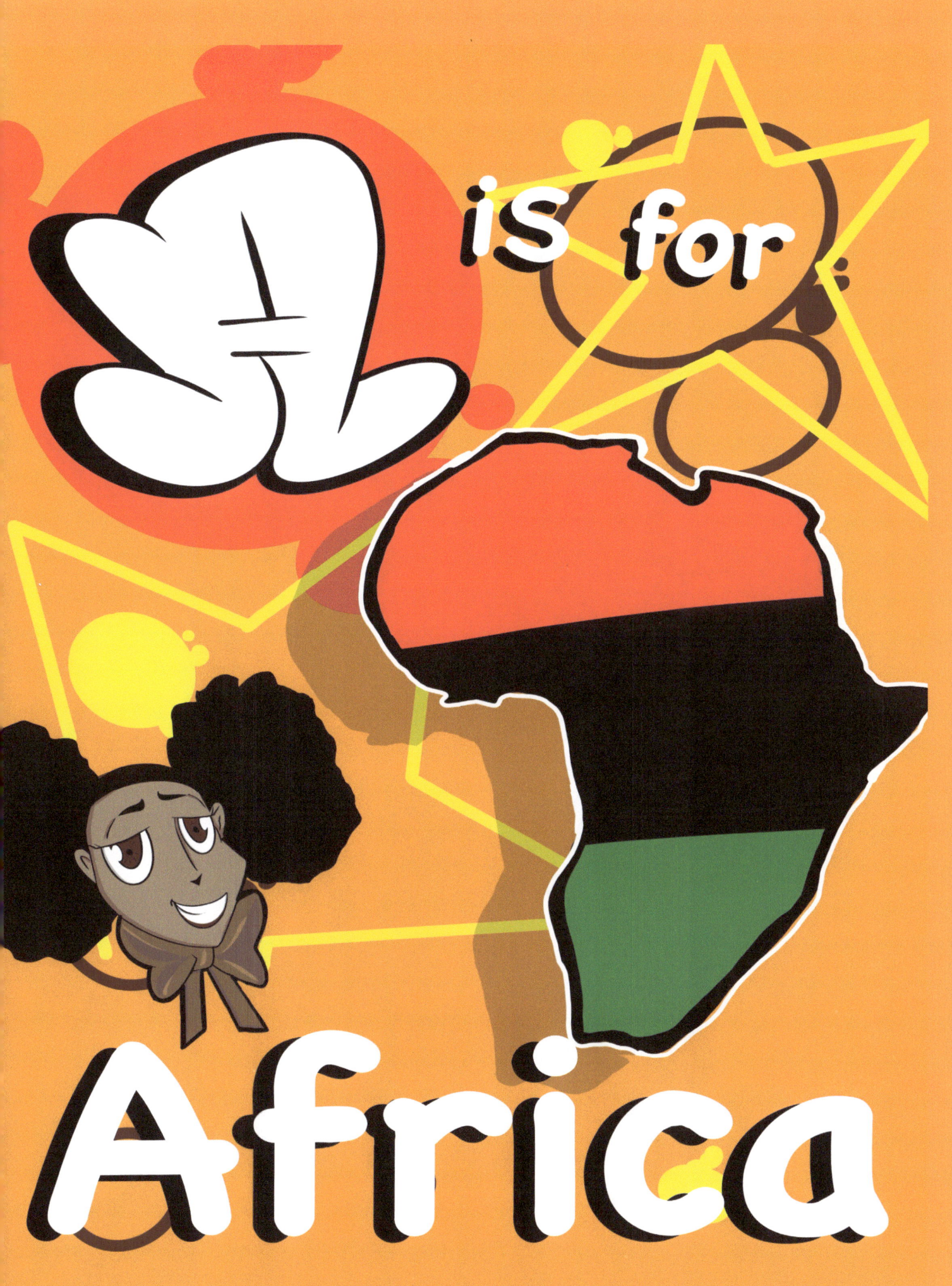

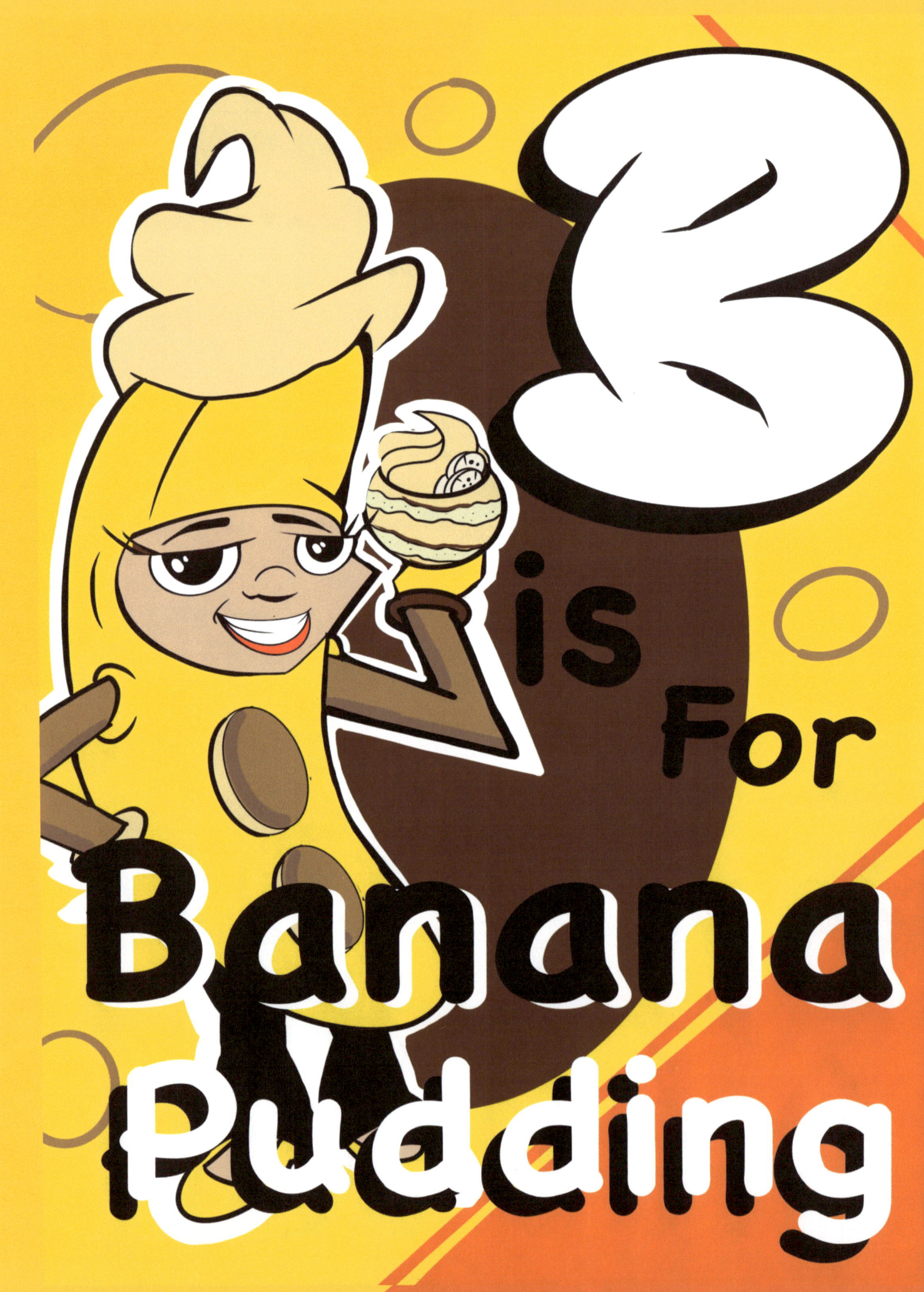

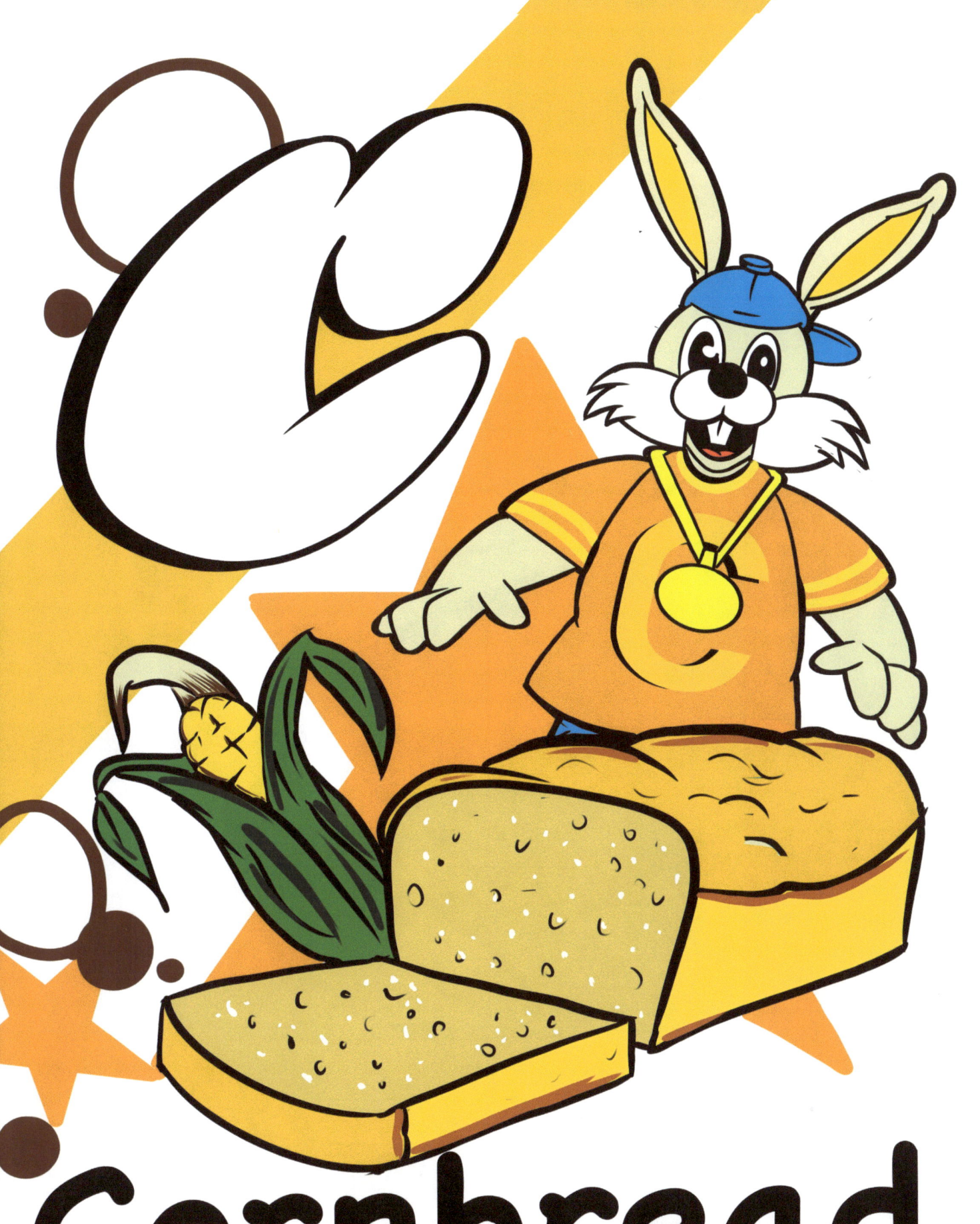

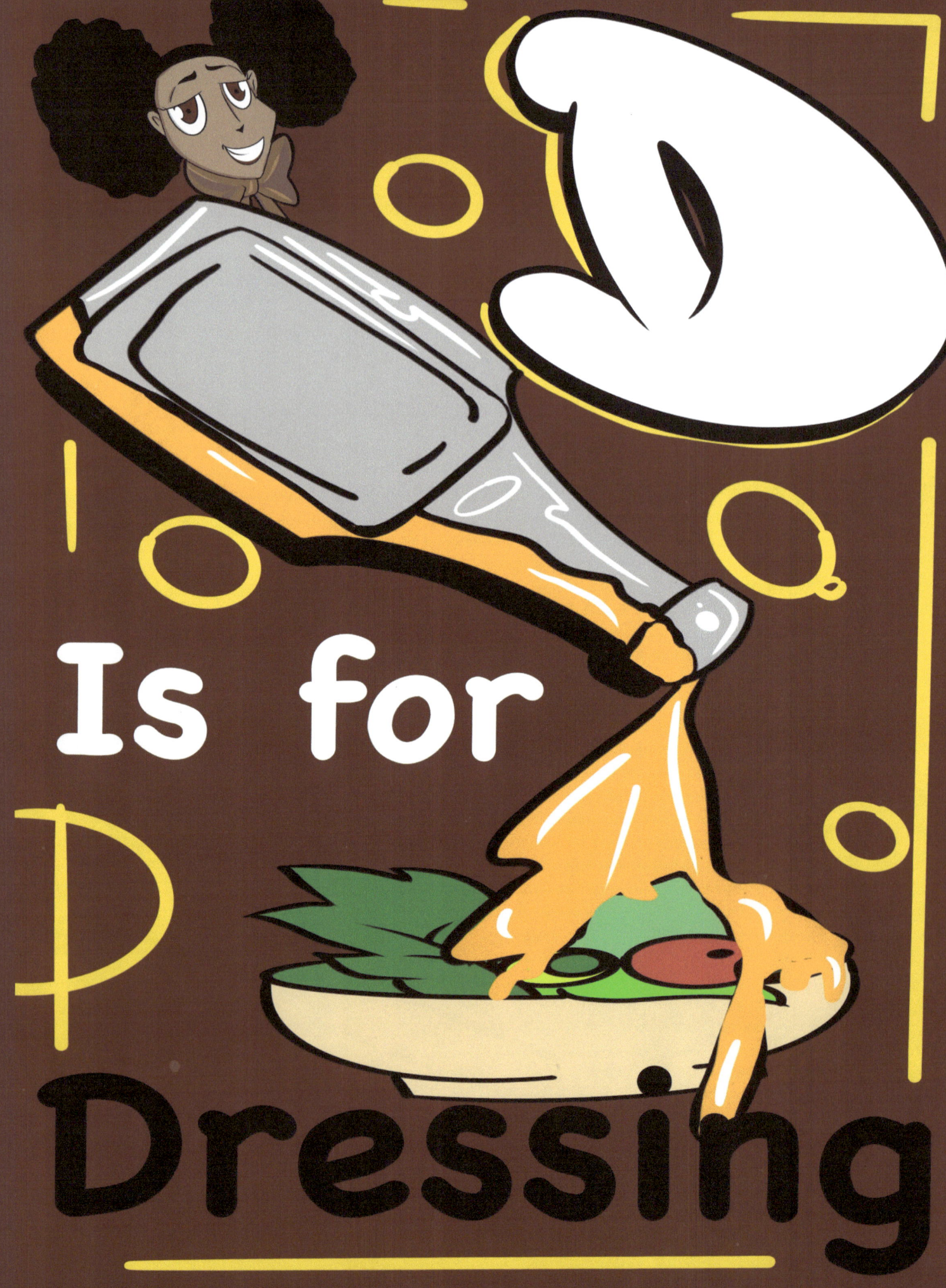

E Is for Egg

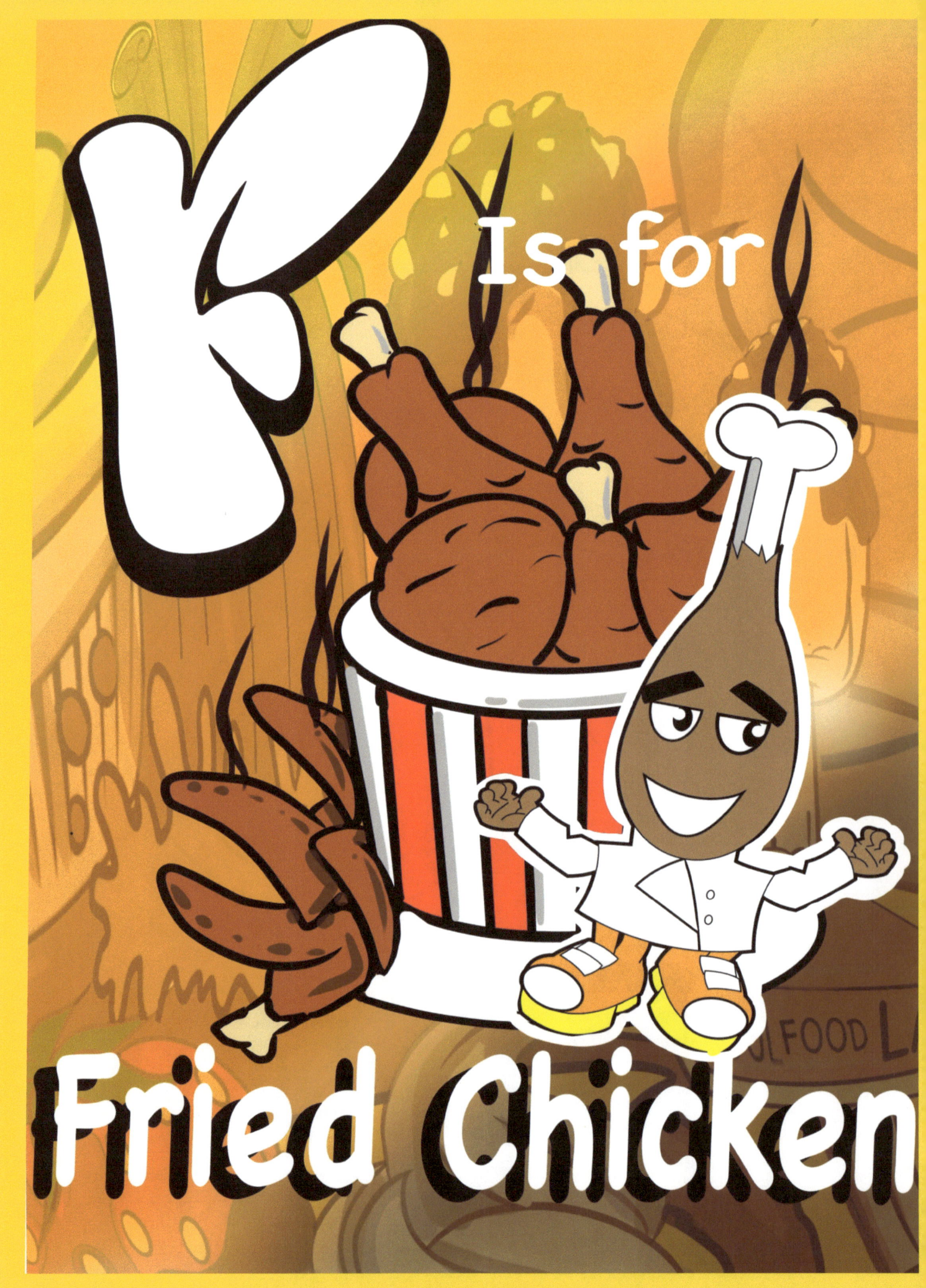

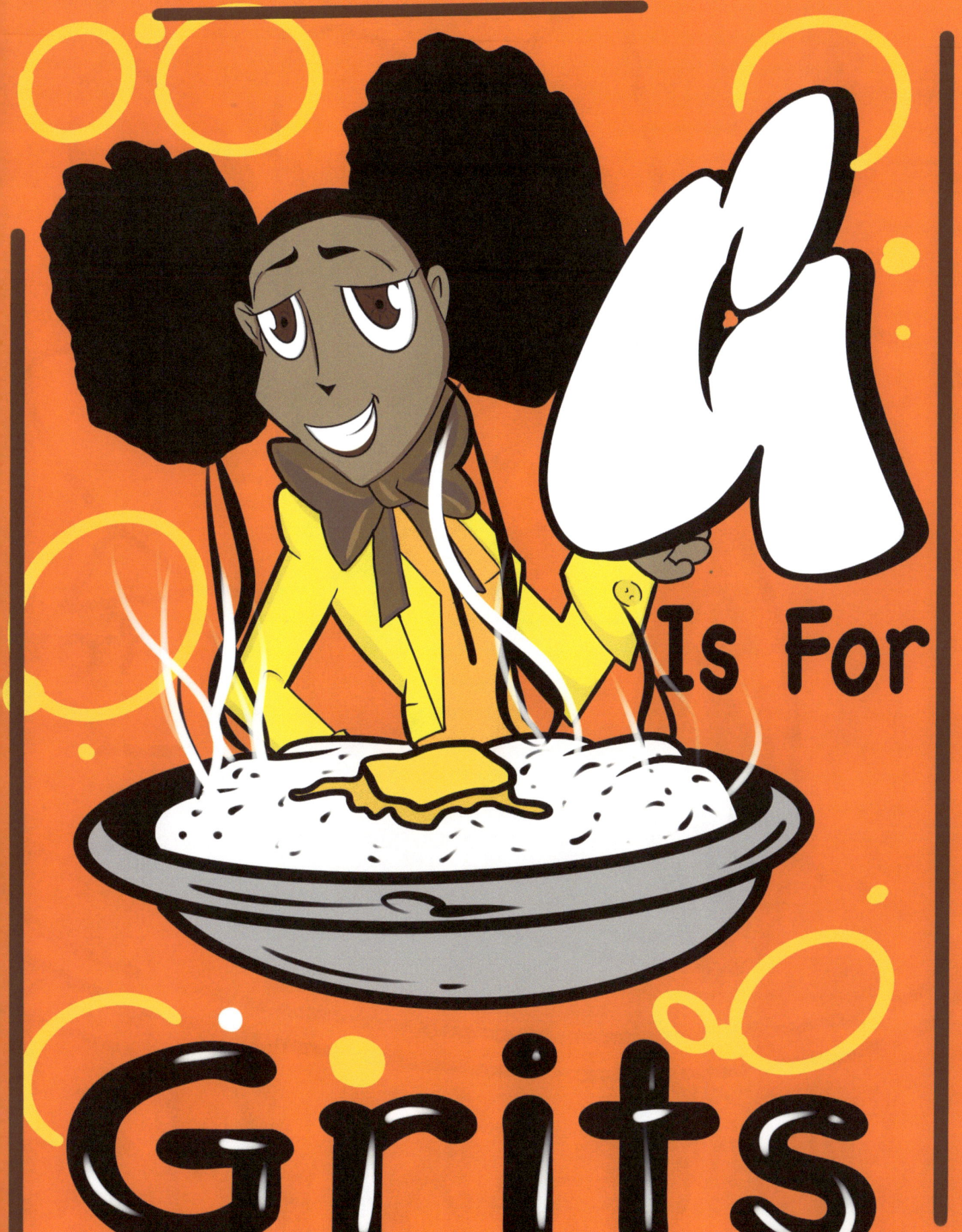

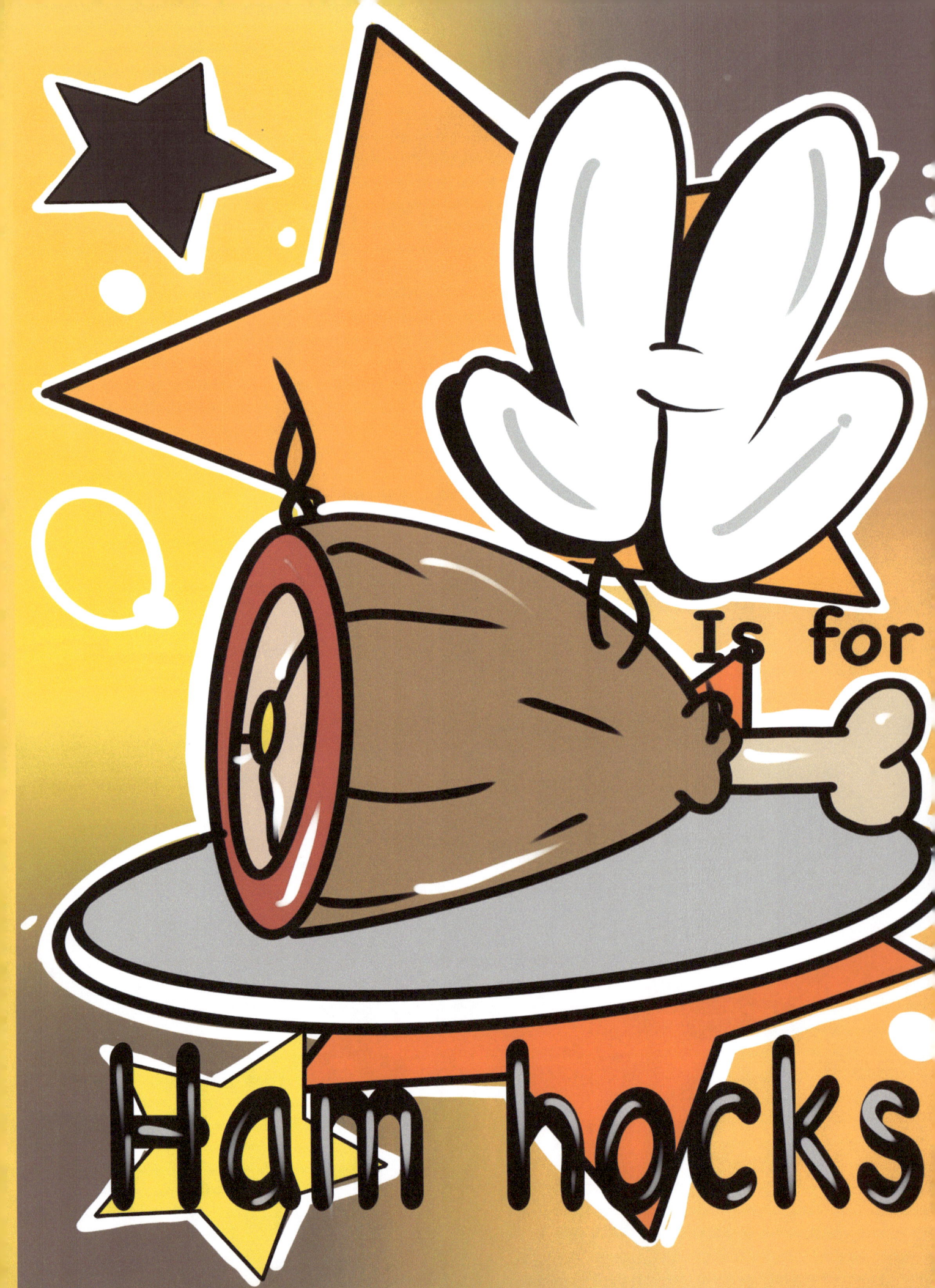

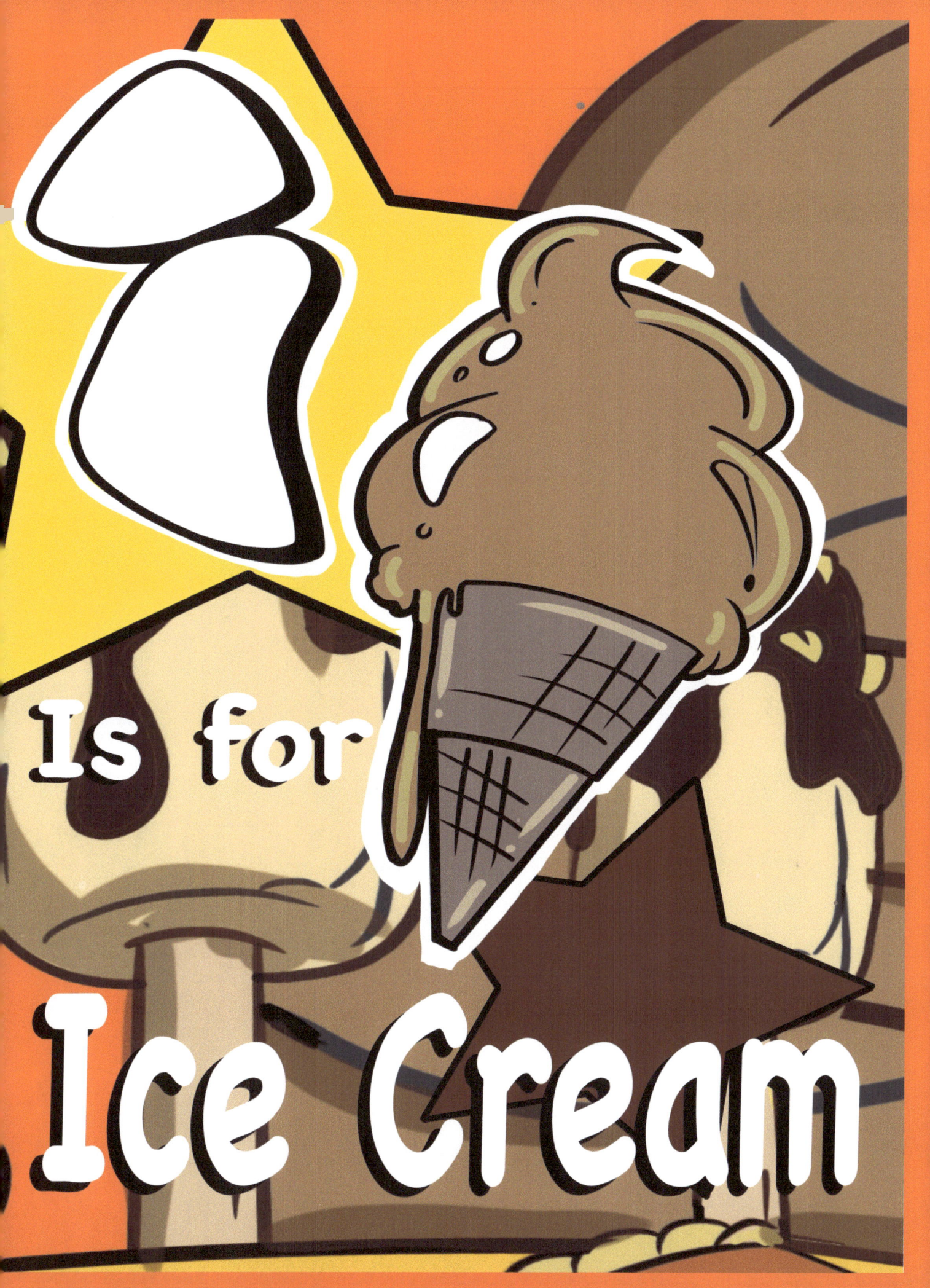

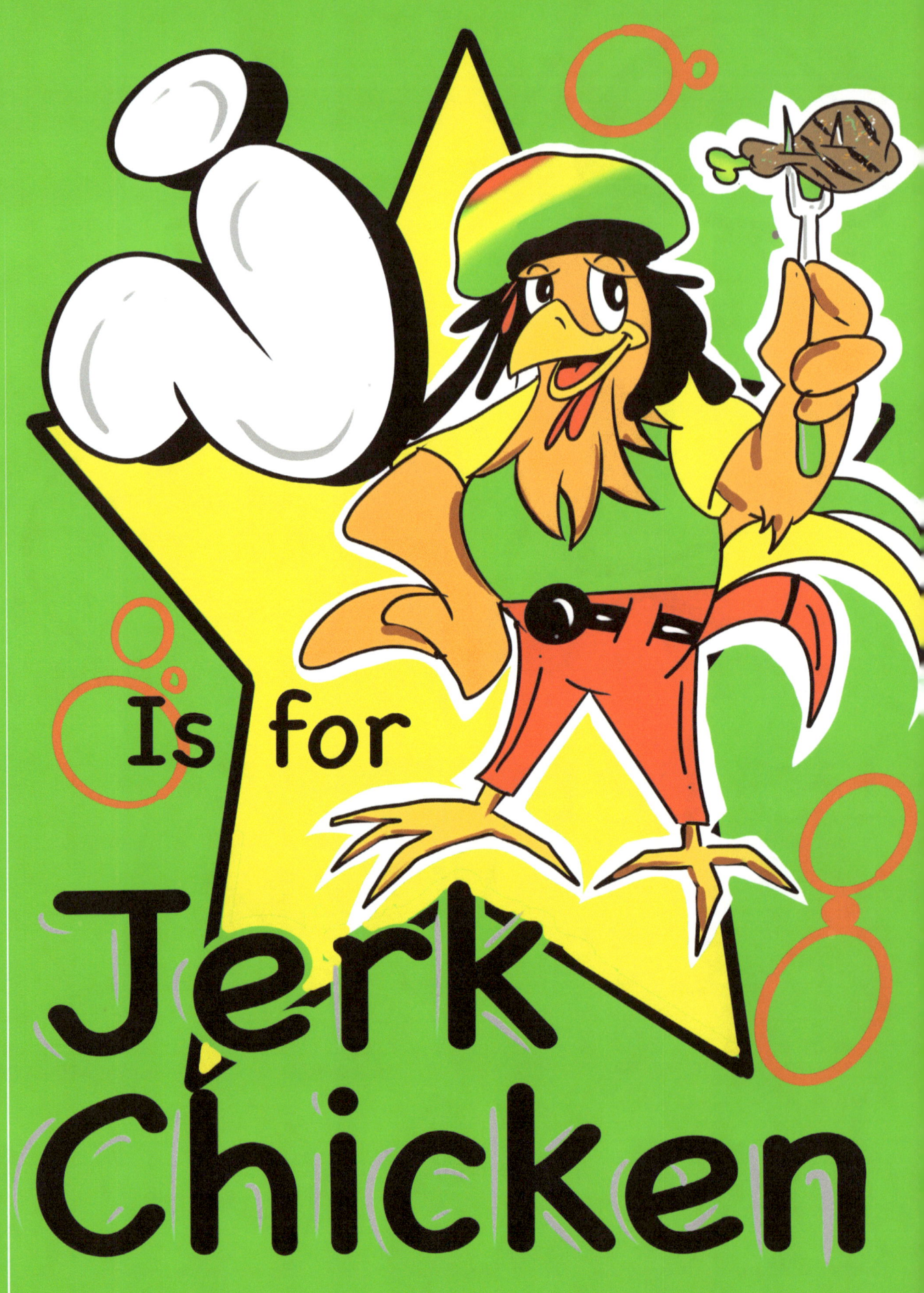

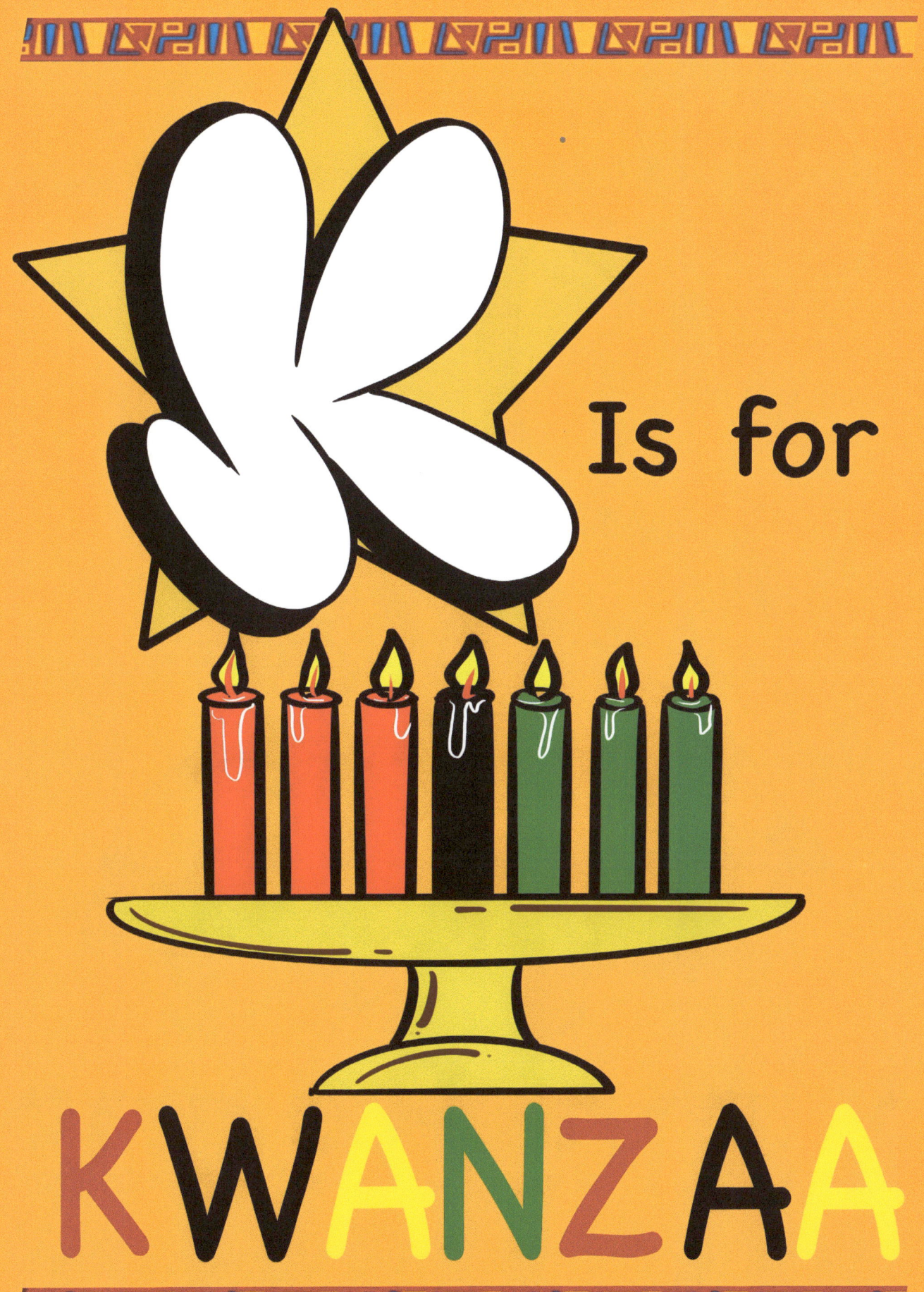

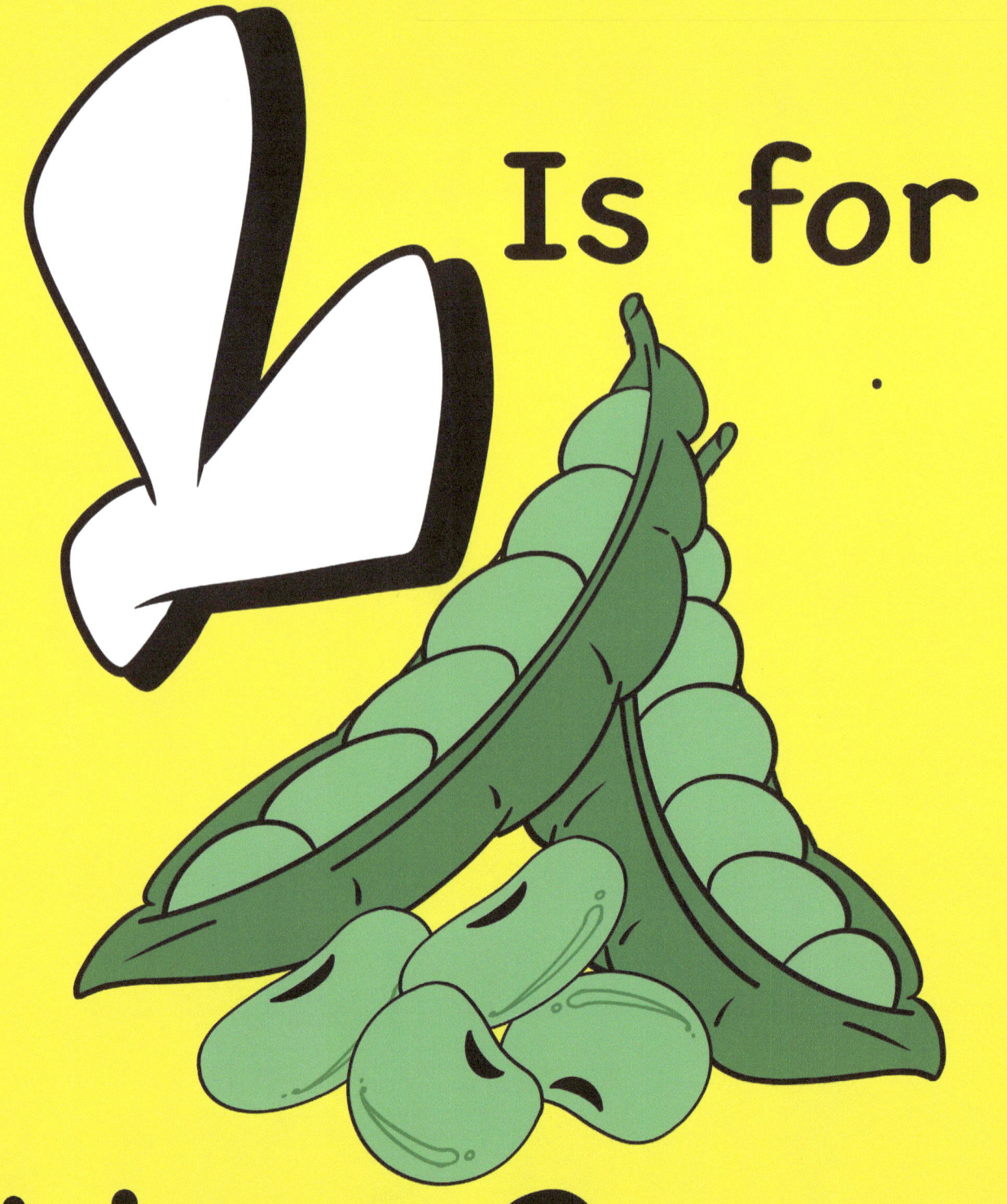

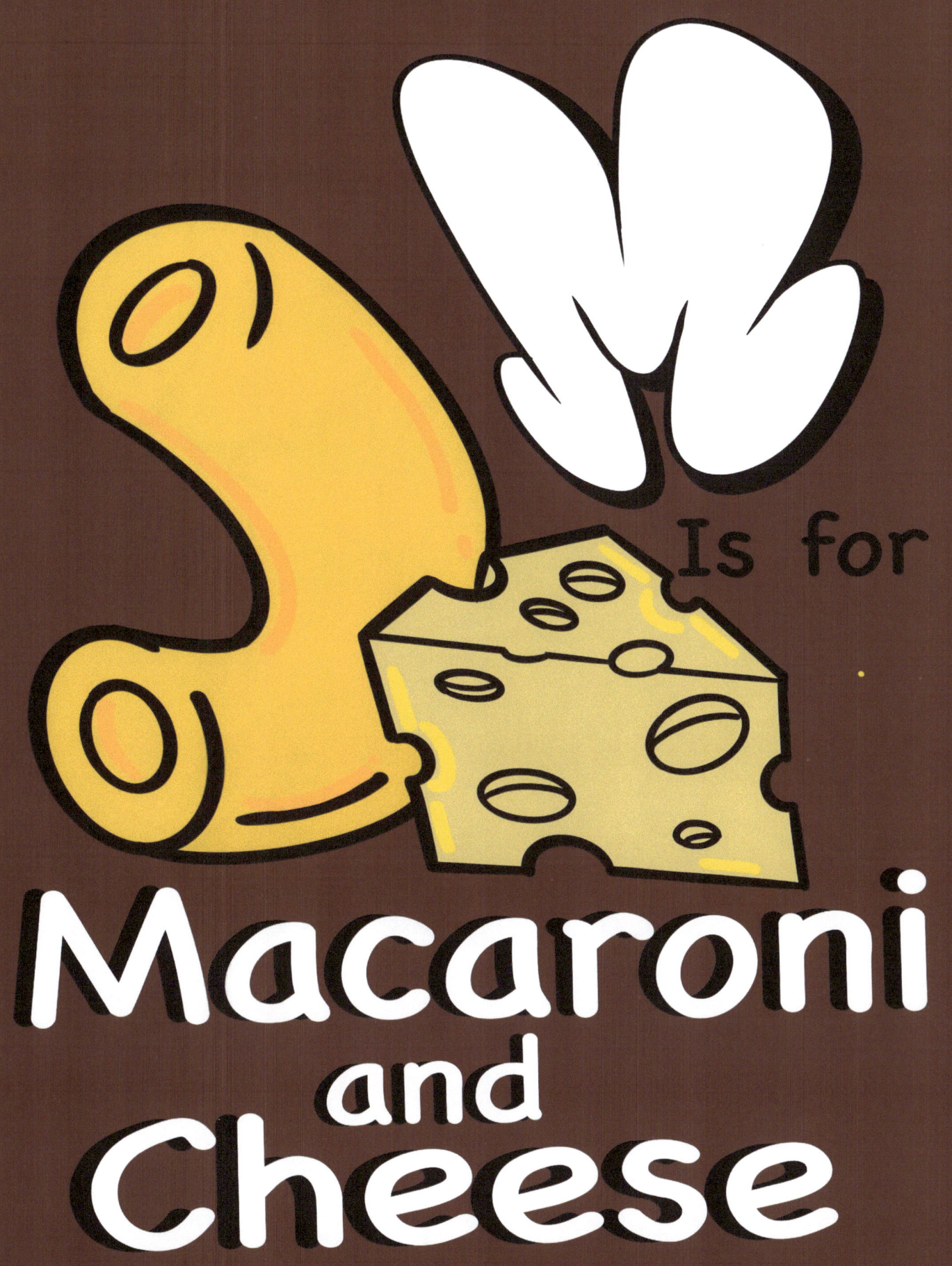

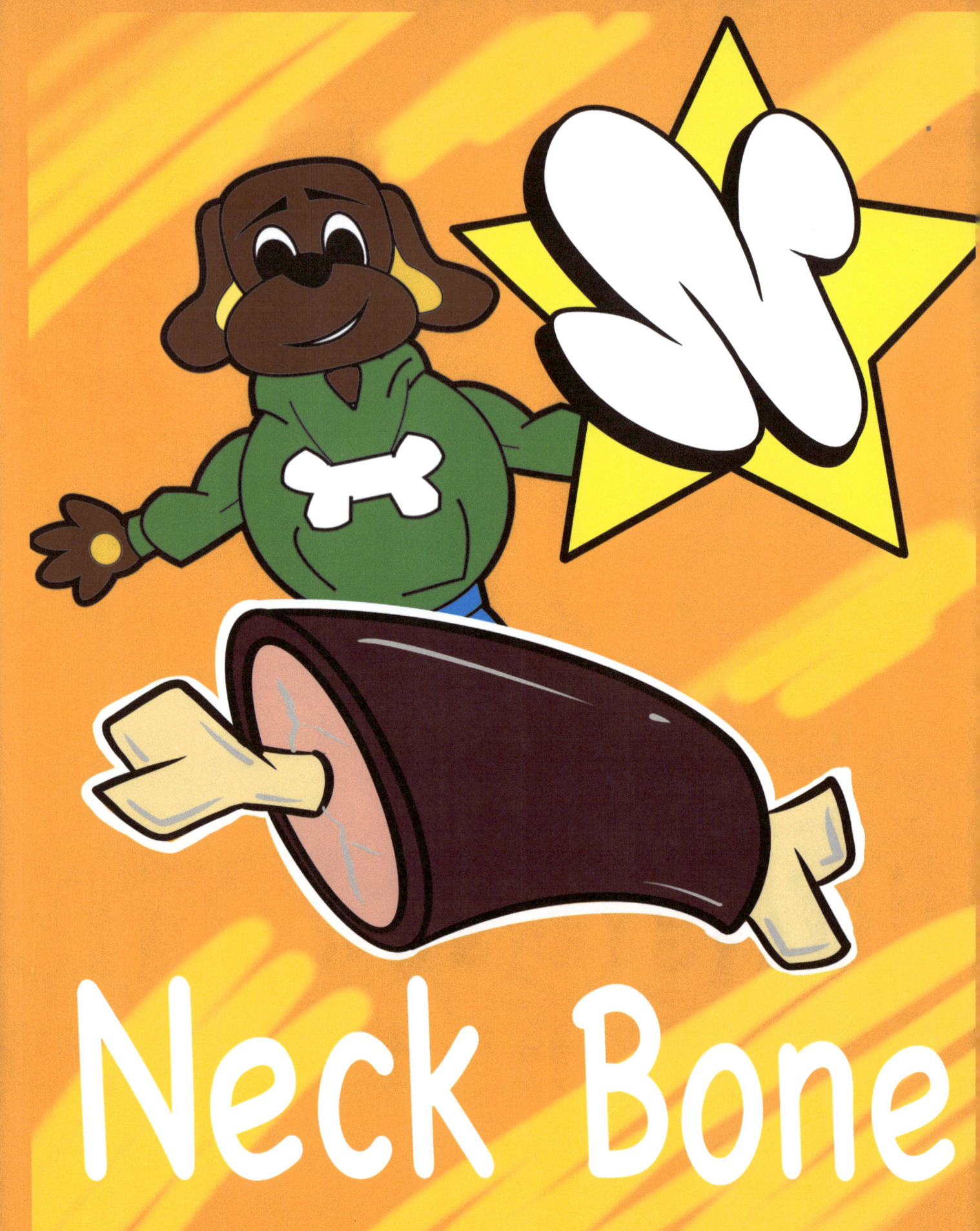

Neck Bone

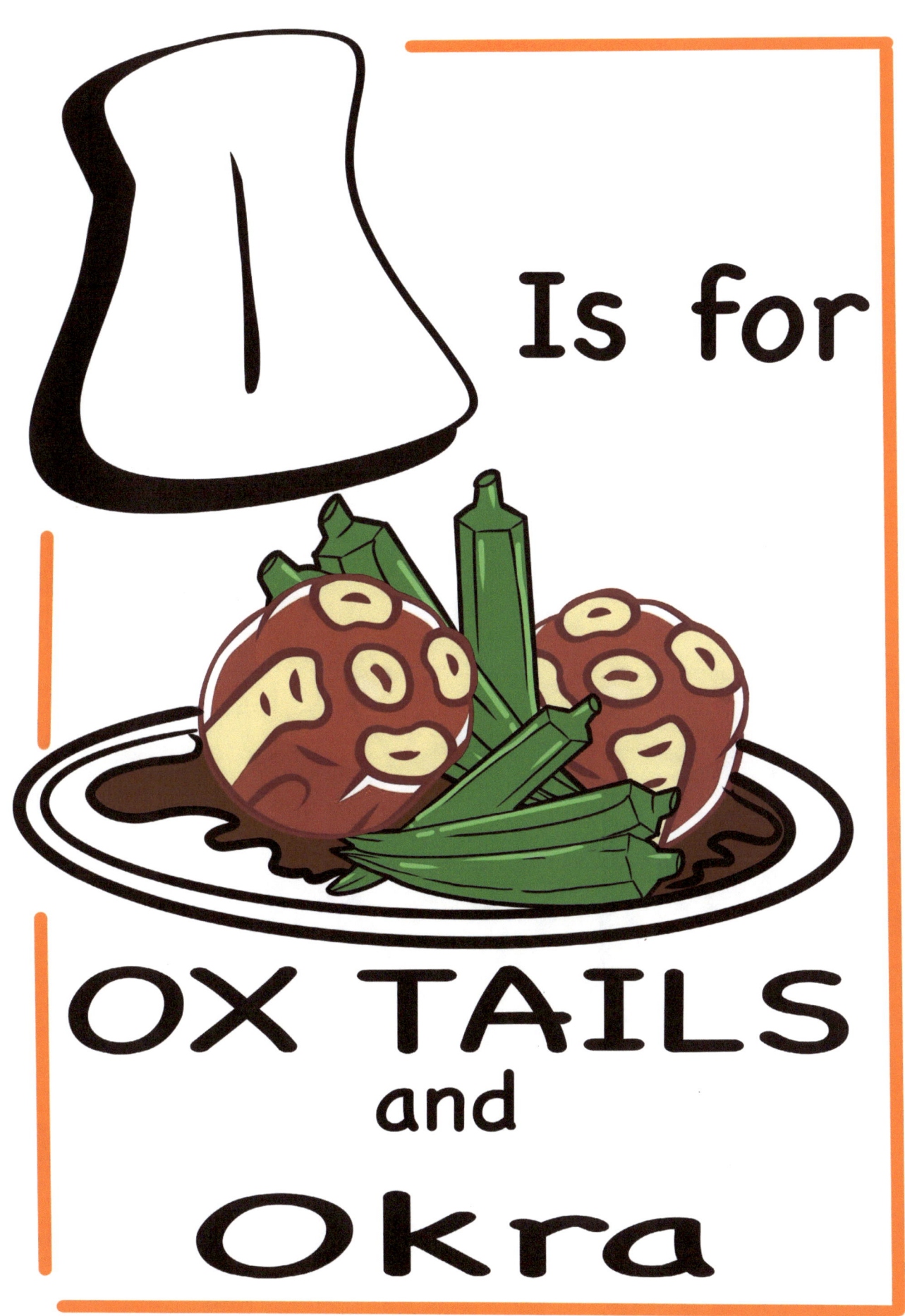

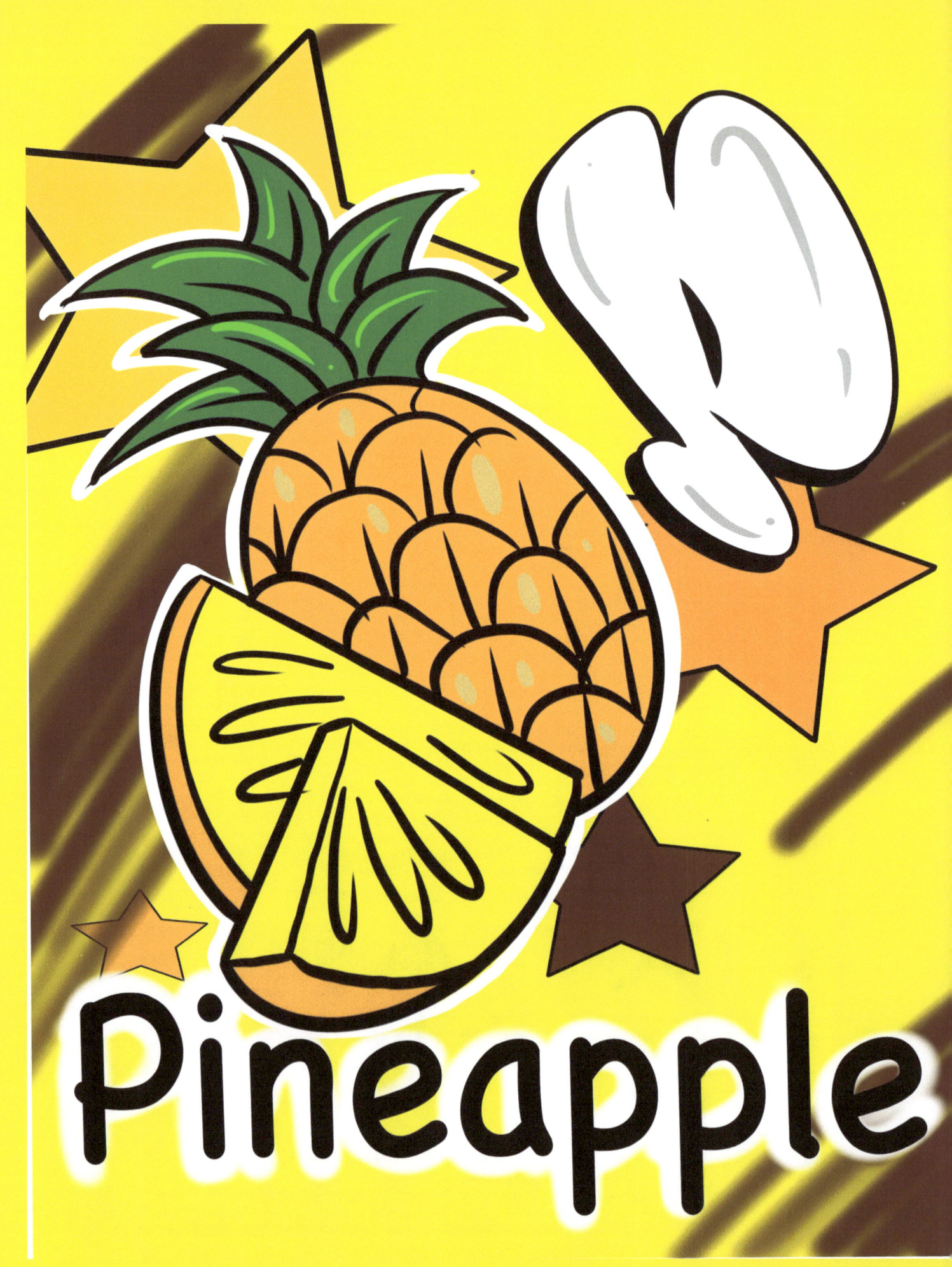

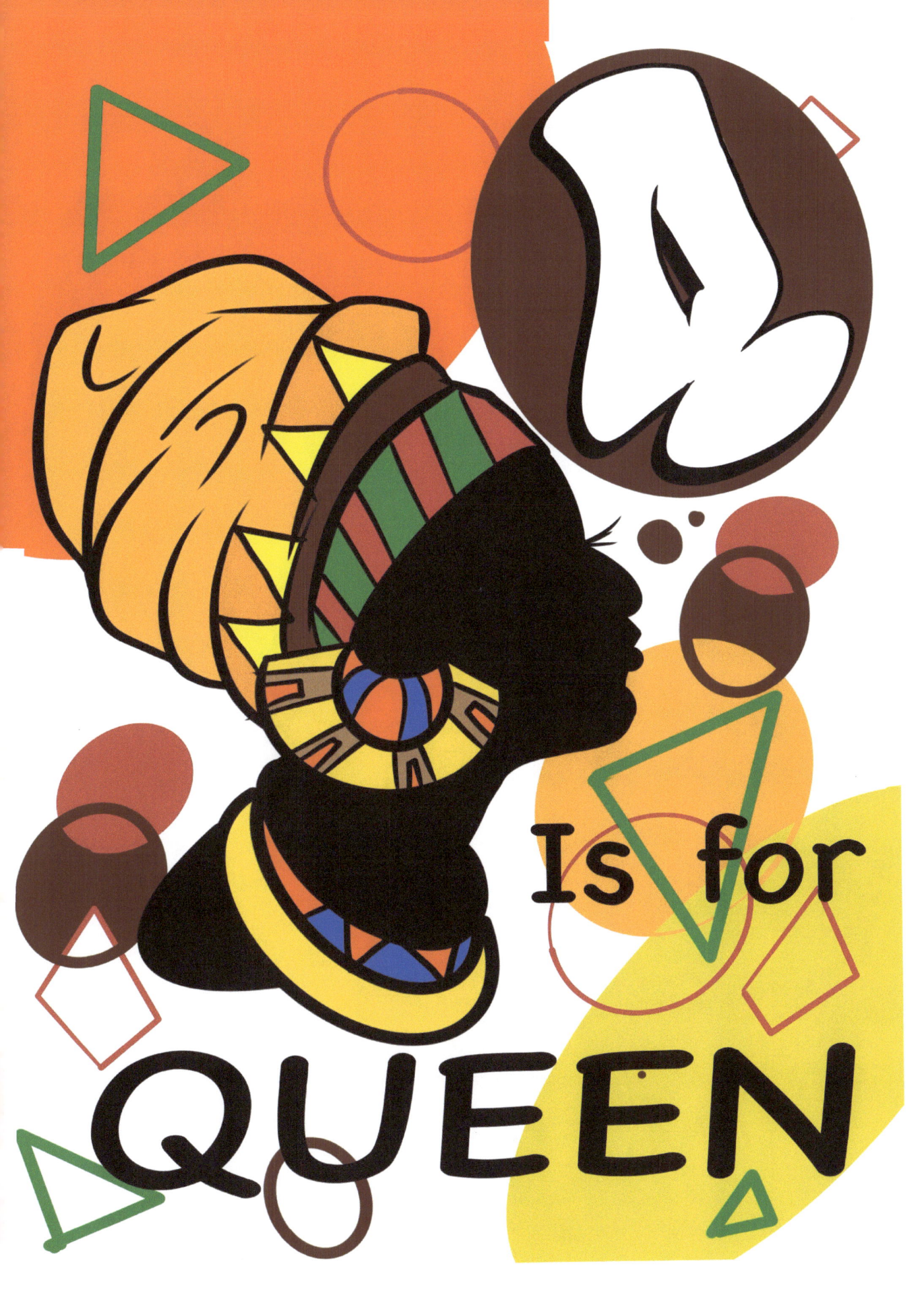

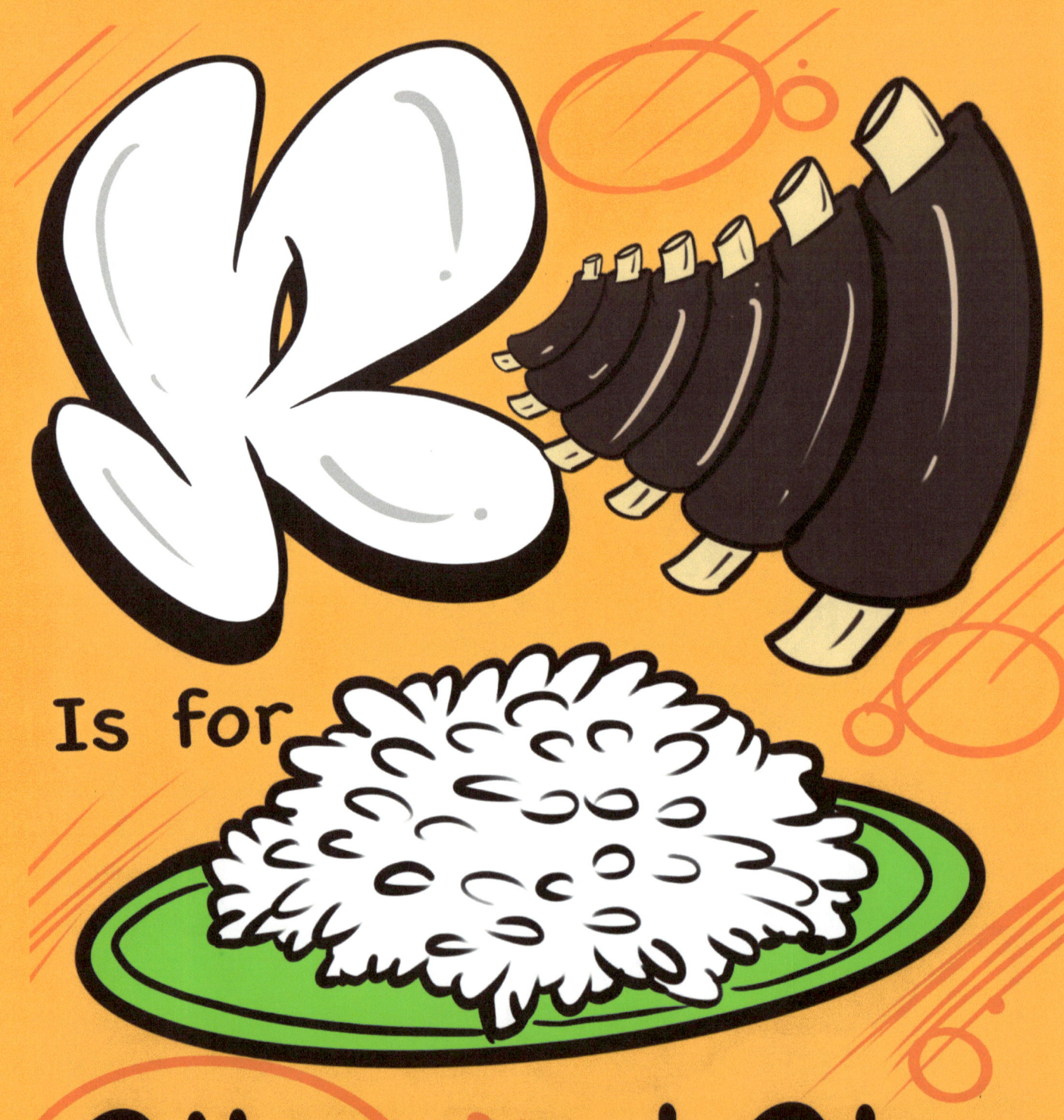

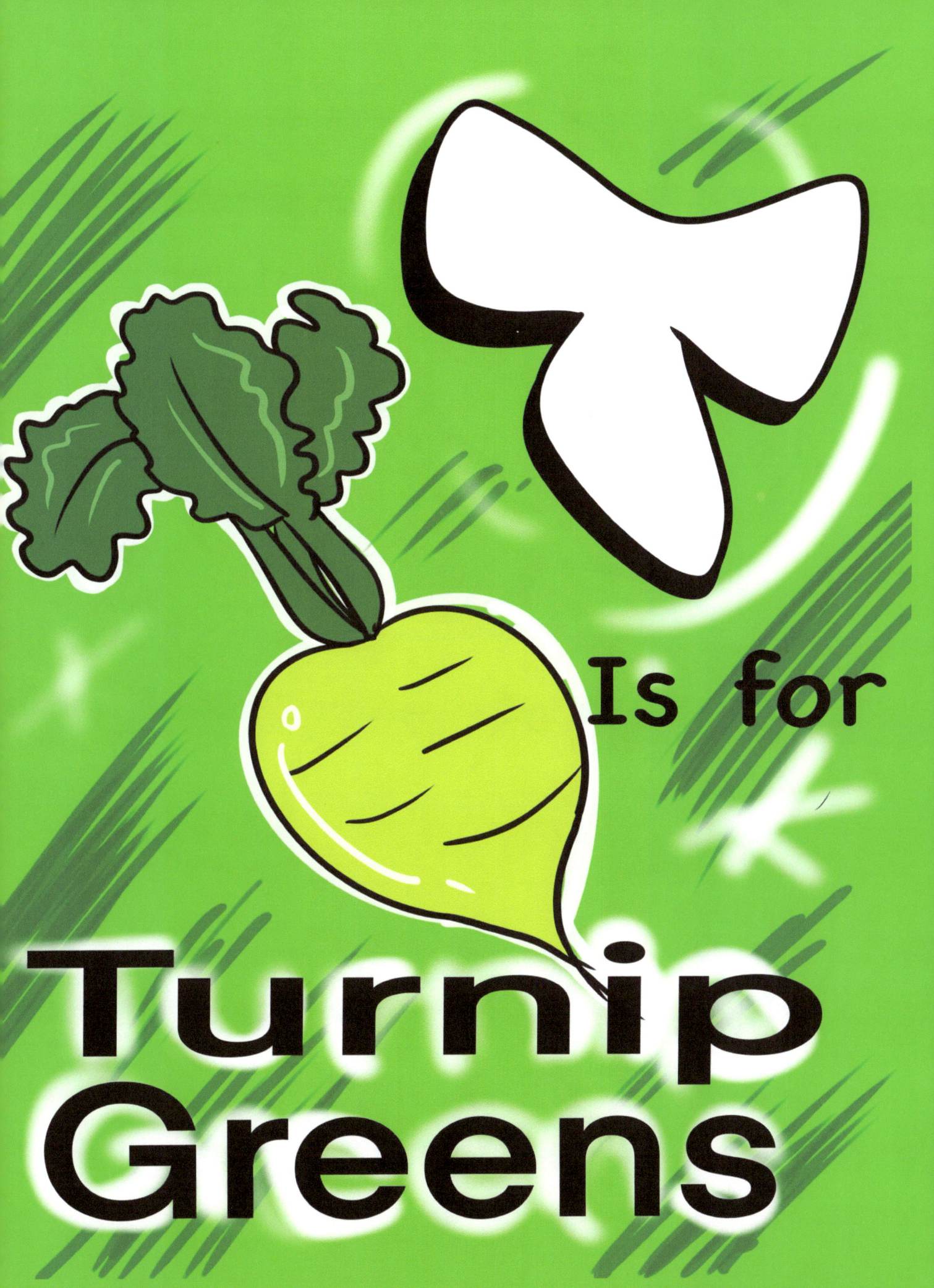

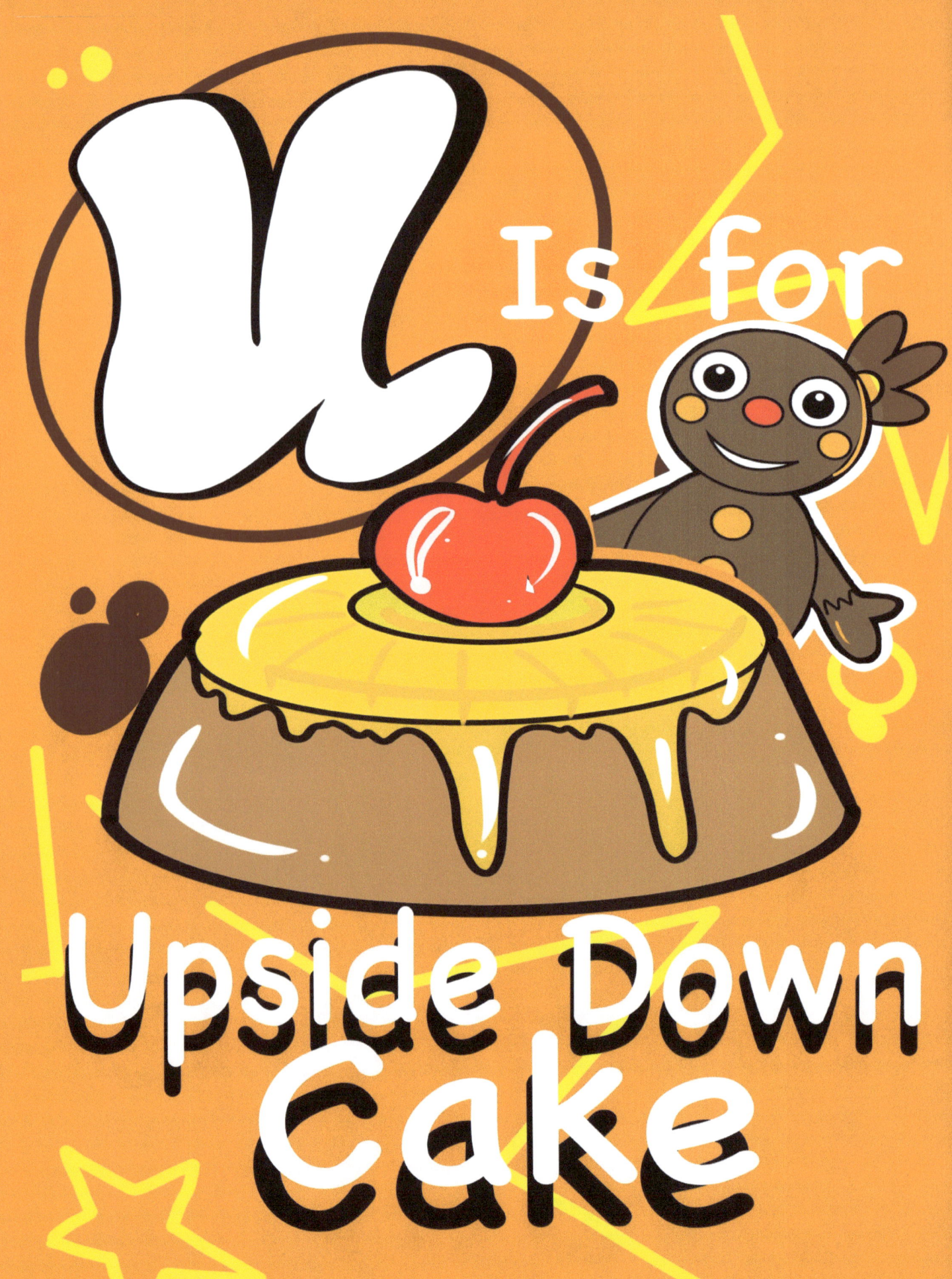

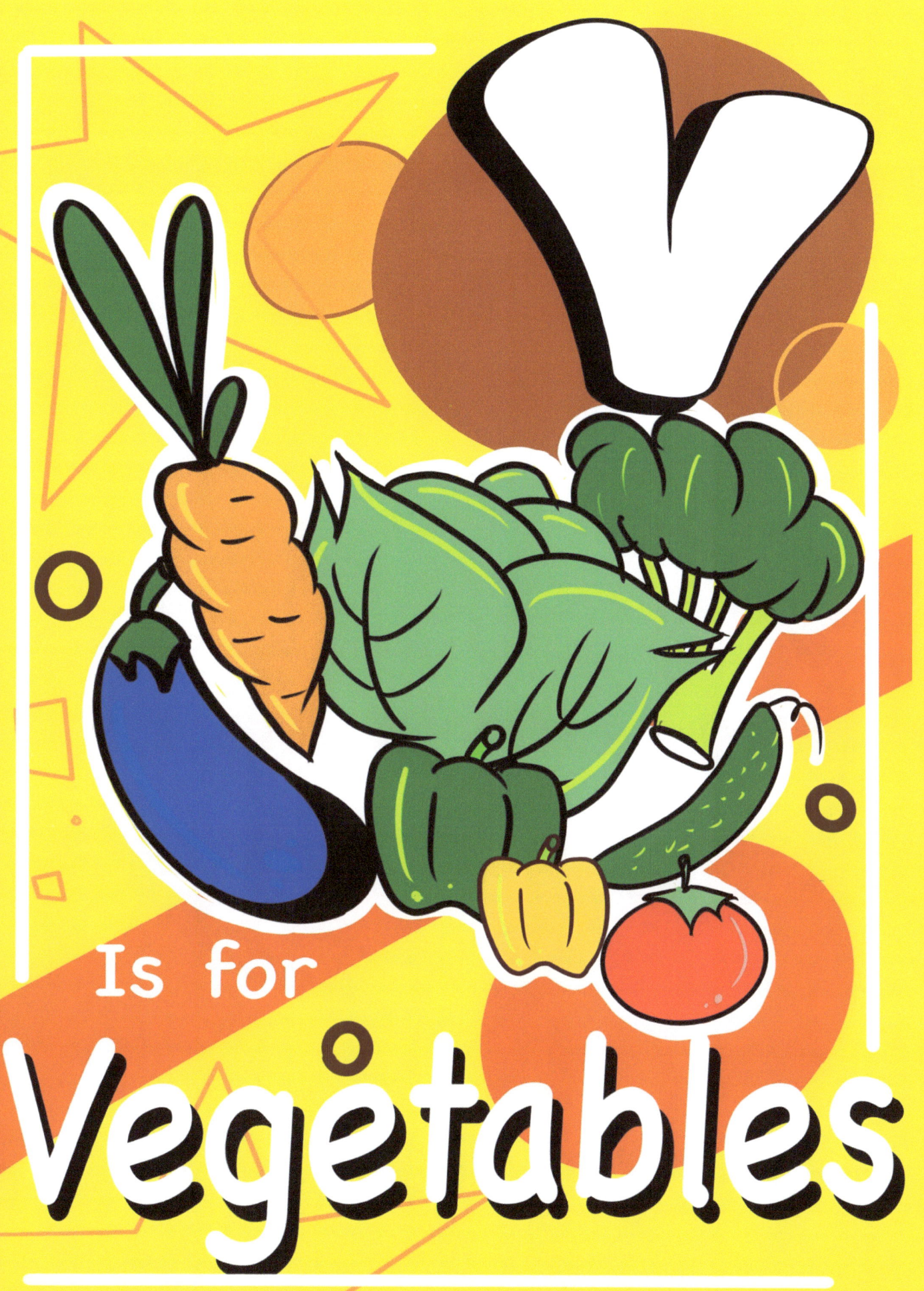

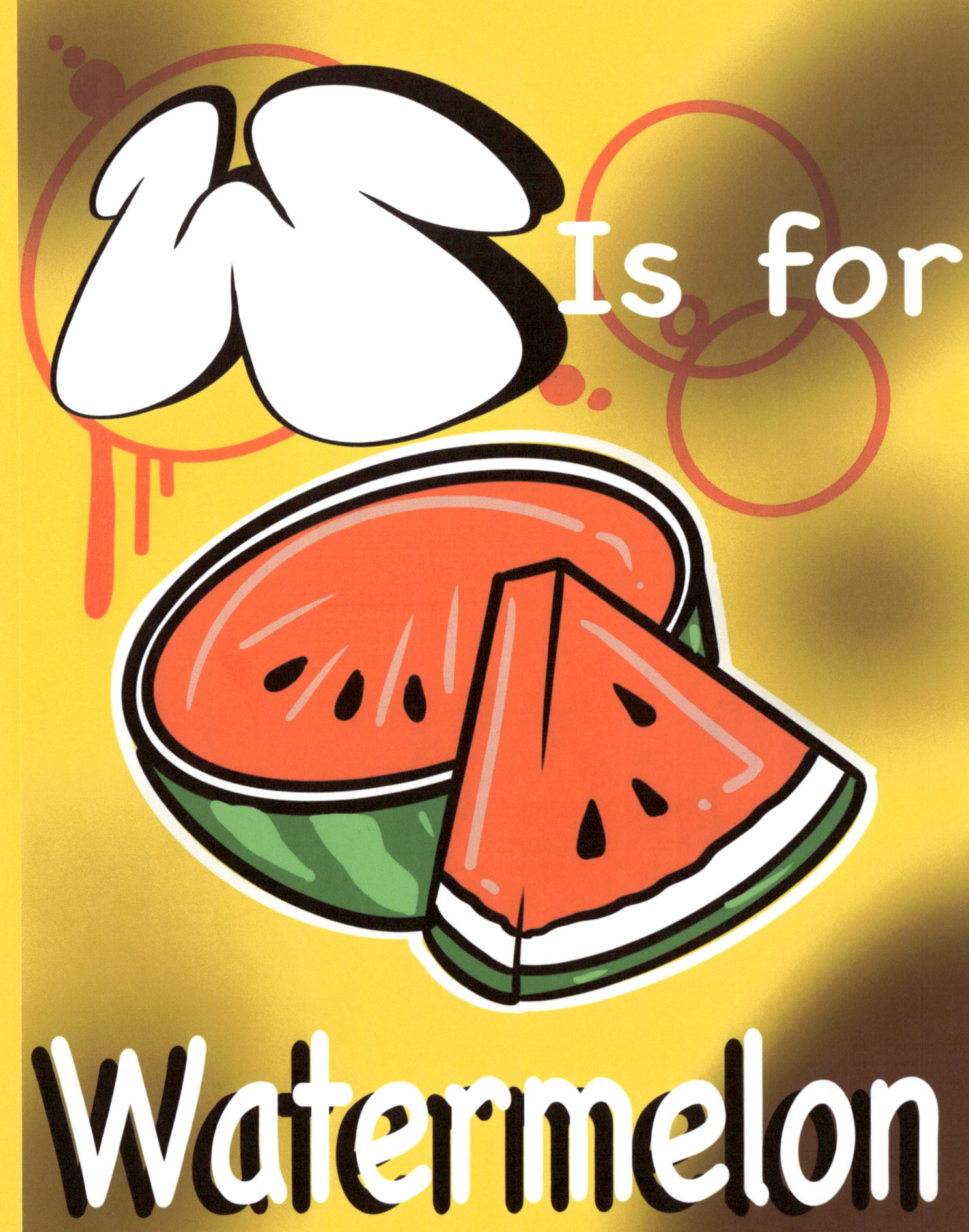

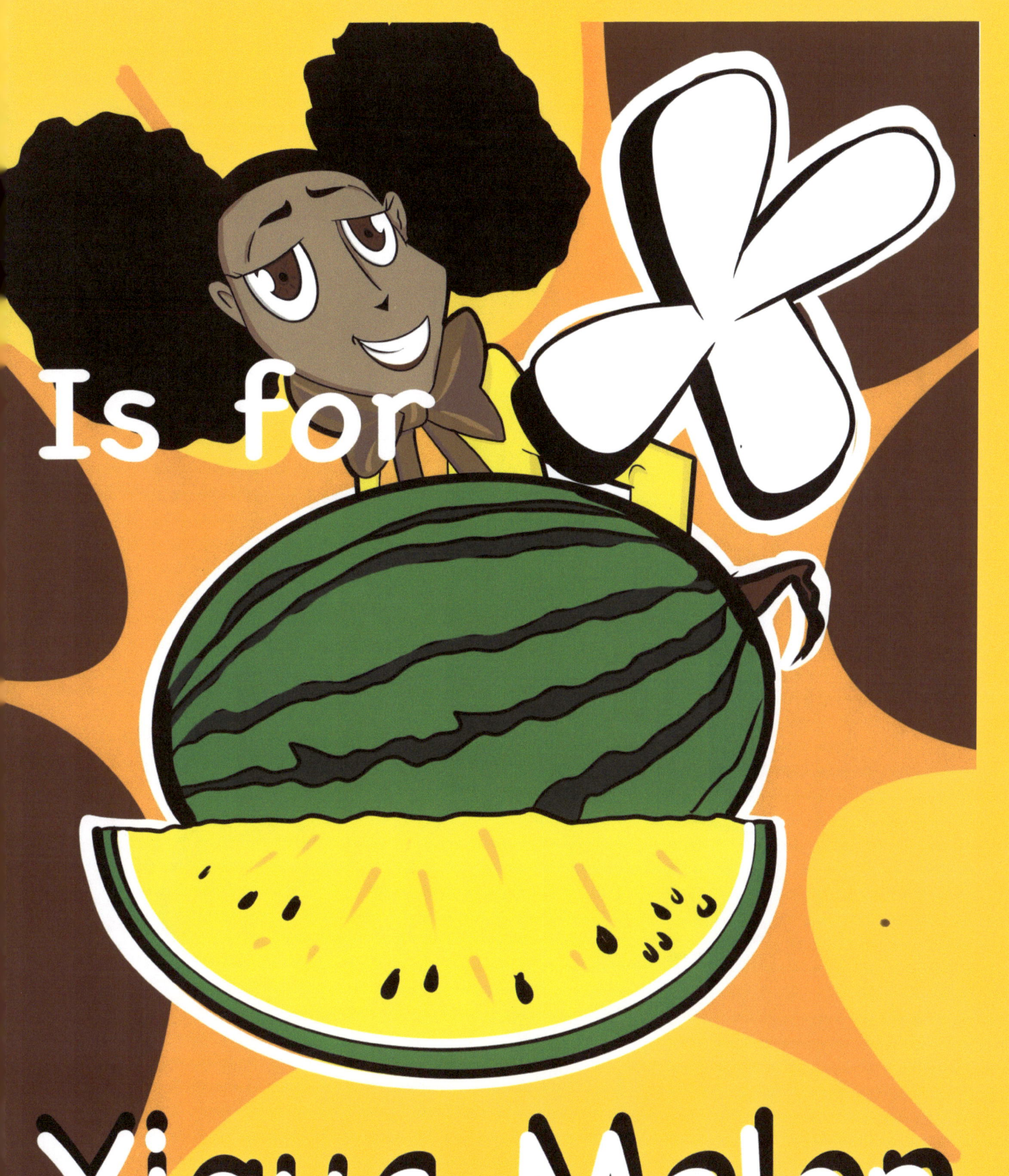

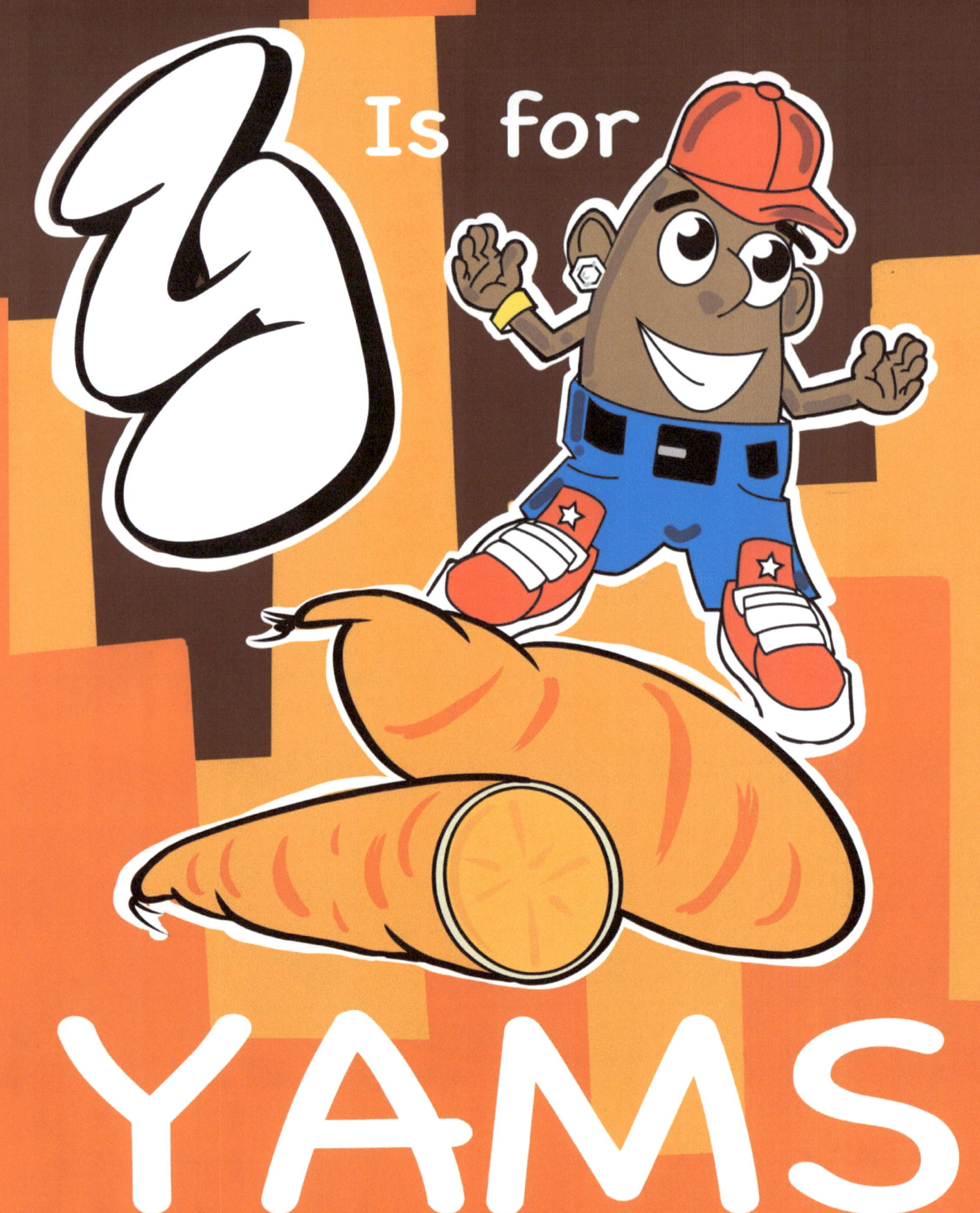

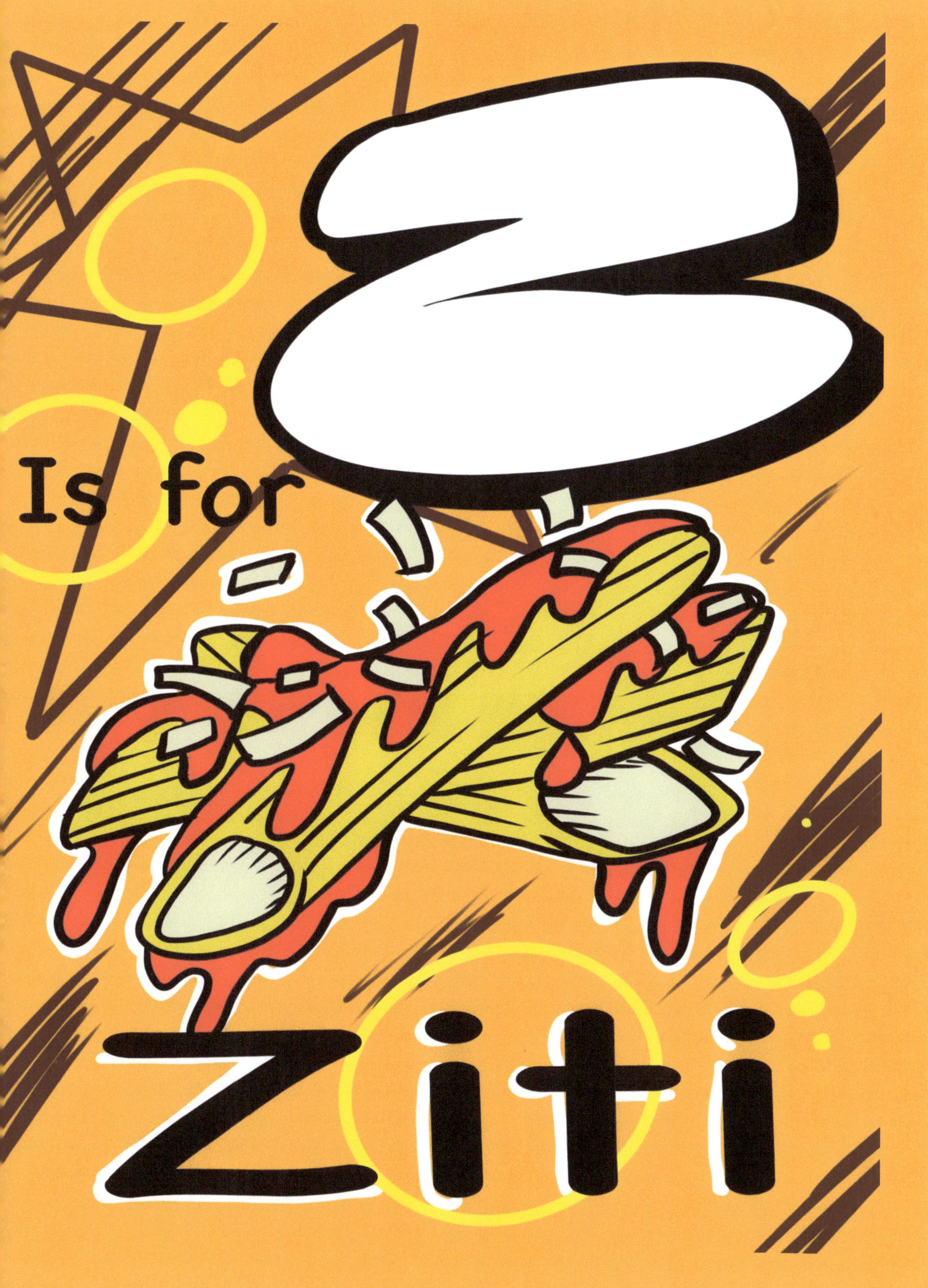